ICT

# What If?

## Anne Rooney

QED Publishing

First published in the UK in 2004 by
QED Publishing
A division of Quarto Publishing plc
The Fitzpatrick Building
188–194 York Way, London N7 9QP

A Catalogue record for this book is available from the
British Library.

ISBN 1 84538 041 X

Written by Anne Rooney
Designed by Jacqueline Palmer
Editor Anna Claybourne
Consultant Philip Stubbs
Illustrator John Haslam
Photographer Ray Moller
Models provided by Scallywags

Screenshot credits:
Page 18 top /Zoo Tycoon, Marine Mania, Microsoft
Corporation /bottom Dogz 4, PF Magic, Ubisoft;
page 22 the Met Office.

Creative Director Louise Morley
Editorial Manager Jean Coppendale

Printed and bound in China

The words in **bold** are
explained in the Glossary
on page 31.

# Contents

You've probably made models since you were small, using plastic bricks, cardboard or modelling clay. A model shows us what something looks like and how it works or behaves.

## Computer models

You can also make **models** of a different kind on a computer. Computer models are useful in many areas of life. For example, architects, engineers and designers experiment with models, trying out different designs for buildings, bridges, vehicles and machinery.

## Simulations

A **simulation** is a model of a process, such as a journey or an event. Computer simulations are used to plan trips by spacecraft, to teach pilots to fly planes, and to practise or experiment with other dangerous or expensive activities.

## Spreadsheets

Governments and businesses use computers to model and plan spending and changes in society. Many of these models are made using spreadsheets – computer programs for working with numbers.

Work out how much money you can raise from a sponsored skate-boarding day.

You can use computers to make models too. In this book, you'll find out how to use spreadsheets to model different situations, and see what happens when you change the numbers.

Find out how much paint you will need to buy to redecorate your room.

You'll also find out how to make a computer model do sums for you, how to put your results into a graph, and even how simulations and spreadsheets can help to forecast the future.

# How does it work?

Spreadsheets are computer documents used for working with numbers. They let you make lots of calculations easily, and update all the answers instantly if you make any changes. They let you work out how things would be if you were to change any aspect of your plan.

## Rows of cells

A spreadsheet has rows of **cells**. Each cell on a spreadsheet is a rectangle in a grid. A cell can hold a number, some words or an instruction to do a calculation. An empty spreadsheet looks something like this:

A row

A cell

A column

We refer to each cell using the letter at the top of the column and the number at the start of the row. So the first cell is A1, the cell to the right of it is B1 – and so on.

When it's being used, a spreadsheet looks like this:

|   | A | B | C | D | E |
|---|---|---|---|---|---|
| 1 | **Pocket money modeller** | | | | |
| 2 | | | | | |
| 3 | Alex gets | | £ 2.50 | | |
| 4 | Fiona gets | | £ 3.50 | | |
| 5 | | | | | |
| 6 | A remote controlled car costs | | | | |
| 7 | £ 40.00 | | | | |
| 8 | | | | | |
| 9 | It will take Alex | | 16.0 | weeks to save | |
| 10 | It will take Fiona | | 11.4 | weeks to save | |
| 11 | | | | | |

## Plan your spending

This spreadsheet is a model of how someone might spend £10 of birthday money. It lists three items and their prices. The spreadsheet adds up the prices to give a total in a separate cell.

|   | A | B | C |
|---|---|---|---|
| 1 | **Birthday money** | | |
| 2 | | | |
| 3 | Pencil case | £3.50 | |
| 4 | Gel pens | £3.50 | |
| 5 | Trading cards | £2.50 | |
| 6 | | | |
| 7 | **Total** | **£9.50** | |
| 8 | | | |

## Making changes

Spreadsheets are useful because you can change the numbers and see different results. For example, if you were to change the second item from pens to a book, the computer would work out the sum again:

|   | A | B | C |
|---|---|---|---|
| 1 | **Birthday money** | | |
| 2 | | | |
| 3 | Pencil case | £3.50 | |
| 4 | Book | £3.99 | |
| 5 | Trading cards | £2.50 | |
| 6 | | | |
| 7 | **Total** | **£9.99** | |
| 8 | | | |

# Make your own spreadsheet

The easiest way to see how a spreadsheet works is to make your own. Here's how to make a simple one about you and your friends' heights.

## Words and numbers

Using your spreadsheet software, start a new spreadsheet and click in the first cell. Type in the title:

How tall are we?

In the cells underneath, type a list of your friends' names. In the cell to the right of each name, put each person's height in centimetres (you can guess if you don't know).

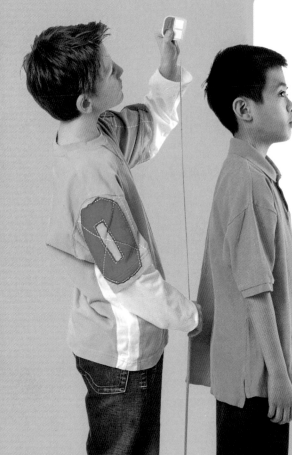

|   | A | B | C |
|---|---|---|---|
| 1 | **How tall are we?** | | |
| 2 | | | |
| 3 | Kate | 124 | |
| 4 | Luki | 122 | |
| 5 | Alex | 135 | |
| 6 | Sarah | 131 | |
| 7 | Max | 136 | |
| 8 | Helena | 129 | |
| 9 | | | |

## Doing sums

So far, you've added text and numbers to the spreadsheet. Now it's time to make it do some work.

Click in cell B9, under the list of heights. Now type

=b3+b4+b5+b6+b7+b8

and press the Enter key.

This tells the spreadsheet to add up the numbers in cells B3–B8. It should change to show how long all of you would be, laid end to end.

|  | A | B | C |
|---|---|---|---|
| 1 | **How long are we?** | | |
| 2 | | | |
| 3 | Kate | 124 | |
| 4 | Luki | 122 | |
| 5 | Alex | 135 | |
| 6 | Sarah | 131 | |
| 7 | Max | 136 | |
| 8 | Helena | 129 | |
| 9 | | 777 | |
| 10 | | | |

If you want to check it, you can lie down with your friends and ask someone to measure you!

### Using symbols

You tell a spreadsheet what to do using simple maths symbols called **operators**. In a spreadsheet, this kind of instruction is called a **formula**.

The equals sign =

tells the computer it has to work out the answer to a sum, and show this in the cell.

The formula we just used...

=b3+b4+b5+b6+b7+b8

...tells the spreadsheet to do a sum by adding the numbers in cells B3, B4, B5, B6, B7 and B8.

Another way to write this formula is

=sum(b3:b8)

This means 'add up all the numbers (find the 'sum' of the numbers) in cells B3 to B8'.

# Working with data

The raw facts and figures that you put into a spreadsheet are called data. What you get out of a spreadsheet is information.

*Yum yum!*

## Where does data come from?

The data you put into a spreadsheet usually comes from the world around you. It might come from a survey, such as asking your friends how many pets they have. Or you could collect data by doing an experiment – for example, by measuring people's heights, the temperature outside or recording the growth of your rabbit.

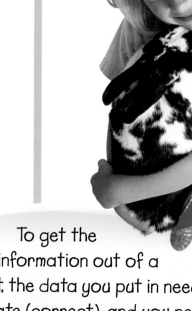

To get the right information out of a spreadsheet, the data you put in needs to be accurate (correct), and you need to make sure you use the right formulas.

## Seed experiment

Imagine you're growing two trays of mustard and cress in two ways. You water one tray every day and the other every three days. Each day, you count how many seeds have sprouted. These measurements are your data.

Tray 1

2 4 9 14 17 17 18

Tray 2

0 2 4 6 7 7 6

You can tell just from this data that the seeds in tray 2 didn't grow as well. But by putting the data into a spreadsheet and making it do some sums, you can find out some more useful information:

|   | A | B | C | D | E | F | G | H |
|---|---|---|---|---|---|---|---|---|
| 1 |   | Day 1 | Day 2 | Day 3 | Day 4 | Day 5 | Day 6 | Day 7 |
| 2 | **Tray 1** | 2 | 4 | 9 | 14 | 17 | 17 | 18 |
| 3 | **Tray 2** | 0 | 2 | 4 | 6 | 7 | 7 | 6 |
| 4 |   |   |   |   |   |   |   |   |
| 5 | **Difference** | 2 | 2 | 5 | 8 | 10 | 10 | 12 |

By subtracting tray 2's numbers from tray 1's numbers, the spreadsheet can show the difference between the trays.

Other symbols are:

**✱** for 'multiply' **/** for 'divide'

## DO IT!

To work out the difference between the trays the formula for cell B5 is:

On day 1:     **=B2-B3**

On day 2:     **=C2-C3**

and so on.

Remember to start each formula with an equals sign.

# Sorting it out

A big spreadsheet can have lots of data in it. It's often easier to spot patterns and find out facts if the data is listed in a particular order. Luckily, a spreadsheet can arrange your data in any order you like.

## Paper problems

Suppose you'd listed the heights of a group of people on paper. You might write them down in the order in which you measured people. So if you wanted to find the tallest person, you'd have to check every number on the list. That's easy with a short list – but what if you'd listed everyone in your school?

How tall are we?

| | |
|---|---|
| | 122 |
| Luki | 124 |
| Kate | 129 |
| Helena | 131 |
| Sarah | 135 |
| Alex | 136 |
| Max | |

How tall are we?

| | |
|---|---|
| Alex | |
| Helena | 135 |
| Kate | 129 |
| Luki | 124 |
| Max | 122 |
| Sarah | 136 |
| | 131 |

If you wanted to put the list on the notice board in alphabetical order of name, or in order of height, you'd need to copy it all out again.

## All in order

A spreadsheet can **sort** your data in any order you like at the click of a button. So you could put your friends in order of increasing or decreasing height, or in alphabetical order of name. And you can change the list around as many times as you like without having to do any more work!

| | A | | C |
|---|---|---|---|
| 1 | **Where we come from** | | |
| 2 | | **Class 5B** | |
| 3 | UK | 20 | |
| 4 | USA | 2 | |
| 5 | Africa | 3 | |
| 6 | Italy | 2 | |
| 7 | Sweden | 1 | |
| 8 | | | |
| 9 | | | |

| | A | B | C |
|---|---|---|---|
| 1 | **Longest rivers** | | |
| 2 | | **Km** | |
| 3 | Nile | 6670 | |
| 4 | Amazon | 6404 | |
| 5 | Chang Jiang | 6378 | |
| 6 | Huang He | 5463 | |
| 7 | Ob-Irtysh | 5410 | |
| 8 | Amur | 4415 | |
| 9 | | | |

| | A | B | C |
|---|---|---|---|
| 1 | **Favourite drinks** | | |
| 2 | | **Votes** | |
| 3 | Cola | 10 | |
| 4 | Lemonade | 7 | |
| 5 | Fruit juice | 6 | |
| 6 | Milkshake | 4 | |
| 7 | Water | 3 | |
| 8 | Tea | 1 | |
| 9 | | | |

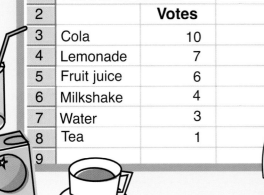

## DO IT!

Look for an option to 'Sort' or 'Order' your data. Pick the column or row you want to use for sorting – such as names or heights. You can also choose whether to sort in ascending order (0–9 or a–z) or descending order (9–0 or z–a).

# Graphs and charts

It's often even easier to see what's going on, and to check your data is correct, if you can see it in the form of a graph or chart. Spreadsheets can do this for you, too.

## Bars, pies and lines

There are several types of graph or chart. You need to pick one that suits what you're doing.

## Bar charts

A **bar chart** is a good way of showing numbers in different categories. This bar chart shows how many birds Luke saw in his garden between 8.00 and 8.30 every day for a week.

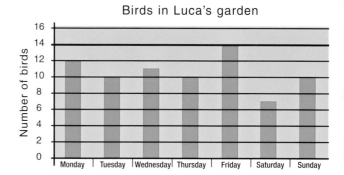

Birds in Luca's garden

Sometimes a chart can help you spot errors in your data. You might need to check your readings, or make sure that you copied the data into the spreadsheet accurately.

## Pie charts

If you want to show proportions, a **pie chart** is best. This pie chart shows how children travel to school. It's easy to see at a glance how the class is divided.

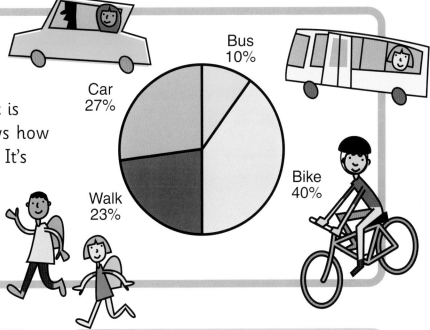

Bus 10%

Car 27%

Bike 40%

Walk 23%

## Pictograms

You can also use a **pictogram**. This shows piles of the things you are counting, such as how many ice-creams you're allowed per week:

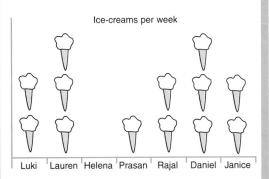

Ice-creams per week

Luki · Lauren · Helena · Prasan · Rajal · Daniel · Janice

## Line graphs

A **line graph** is best if you have data made up of occasional readings. For instance, if you weighed a puppy once a week over three months, you could show the results as a line graph. The puppy grows all the time, but you don't measure it all the time. The line fills in the gaps.

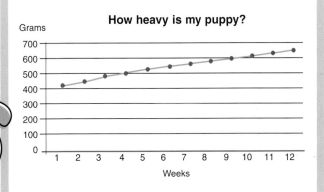

**How heavy is my puppy?**

Grams

700
600
500
400
300
200
100
0

1  2  3  4  5  6  7  8  9  10  11  12

Weeks

# Filtered facts

It's often useful to be able to pick out only some of the information in your spreadsheet. This is called filtering your data.

## In the sun

Here's an example of how you might **filter** useful data. This spreadsheet shows how many hours of sunshine you can expect each day in different holiday resorts during the summer.

| | A | B | C | D | E | F |
|---|---|---|---|---|---|---|
| 1 | Pick a holiday | | | | | |
| 2 | | | | Hours of sunshine in | | |
| 3 | Resort code | Country | June | July | August | September |
| 4 | | | | | | |
| 5 | AB01 | Italy | 9 | 10 | 11 | 9.5 |
| 6 | AB02 | France | 8 | 9.5 | 9.5 | 7.5 |
| 7 | AB03 | Spain | 9 | 10.5 | 11 | 10 |
| 8 | EC01 | Turkey | 10 | 12 | 12 | 11 |
| 9 | EC02 | Spain | 8 | 9 | 10 | 8.5 |
| 10 | EC03 | Turkey | 11 | 12.5 | 12 | 11.5 |
| 11 | RG04 | Italy | 10 | 11 | 11 | 10.5 |
| 12 | RG06 | France | 7 | 8 | 9 | 8 |
| 13 | EW03 | Germany | 6 | 6 | 7 | 6.4 |
| 14 | EW06 | Italy | 9 | 10.5 | 11 | 10 |
| 15 | NU12 | Spain | 8 | 9.5 | 10.5 | 10 |
| 16 | NU14 | France | 7 | 8.5 | 9 | 8 |
| 17 | ZX02 | Italy | 10 | 11.5 | 11 | 10 |
| 18 | ZX03 | Turkey | 10.5 | 11.5 | 12.5 | 11 |

## Where?

If you'd decided to go to Italy, you could ask the spreadsheet to show you only the information for Italy.

| | A | B | C | D | E | F |
|---|---|---|---|---|---|---|
| 1 | Pick a holiday | | | | | |
| 2 | | | | Hours of sunshine in | | |
| 3 | Resort code | Country | June | July | August | September |
| 4 | | | | | | |
| 5 | AB01 | Italy | 9 | 10 | 11 | 9.5 |
| 11 | RG04 | Italy | 10 | 11 | 11 | 10.5 |
| 14 | EW06 | Italy | 9 | 10.5 | 11 | 10 |
| 17 | ZX02 | Italy | 10 | 11.5 | 11 | 10 |

## When?

Or, if you were planning a holiday in August, you could ask your sunshine spreadsheet to show you only resorts that would have more than ten hours of sunshine a day in August.

| | A | B | C | D | E | F |
|---|---|---|---|---|---|---|
| 1 | Pick a holiday | | | | | |
| 2 | | | | Hours of sunshine in | | |
| 3 | Resort code | Country | June | July | August | September |
| 4 | | | | | | |
| 5 | AB01 | Italy | 9 | 10 | 11 | 9.5 |
| 7 | AB03 | Spain | 9 | 10.5 | 11 | 10 |
| 8 | EC01 | Turkey | 10 | 12 | 12 | 11 |
| 9 | EC02 | Spain | 8 | 9 | 10 | 8.5 |
| 10 | EC03 | Turkey | 11 | 12.5 | 12 | 11.5 |
| 11 | RG04 | Italy | 10 | 11 | 11 | 10.5 |
| 14 | EW06 | Italy | 9 | 10.5 | 11 | 10 |
| 15 | NU12 | Spain | 8 | 9.5 | 10.5 | 10 |
| 17 | ZX02 | Italy | 10 | 11.5 | 11 | 10 |
| 18 | ZX03 | Turkey | 10.5 | 11.5 | 12.5 | 11 |

## Making filters

To filter data, you pick the column or row you want to use, then tell the spreadsheet what to look for. You can ask for exact matches, or a range of data.

You need to use **operators** to tell the spreadsheet the range of numbers you want to look for. If you chose the 'August' column, for example, you could then use these operators to filter the data:

### equals =

**=10**

will find all resorts that expect exactly ten hours of sunshine

### more than >

**>10**

will find resorts with more than ten hours of sunshine

### less than <

**<10**

will find resorts with less than ten hours of sunshine

## DO IT!

Look for an option to 'Filter' your spreadsheet. You might be able to choose more than one thing to look for – for example:

**Country = Italy AND August =>10**

would look for resorts in Italy that had ten or more hours of sunshine a day in August.

# Simulations

A simulation is a model of a real-life event or process. You might have played computer games that are simulations.

## Types of simulations

There are lots of different types of simulation games – driving, flying a spaceship, keeping pets, building empires...

A simulation game might let you build and manage an imaginary zoo...

Or keep just one little virtual pet.

A simulation isn't as complicated as real life, but it can still be a very useful place to practise.

## Imaginary worlds

Simulations aren't just for fun. They can be used to teach people real, important skills. For example, people learning to fly planes start by learning with simulators, so they can make mistakes safely.

## Spreadsheets for modelling

The type of models in a simulation game are very complicated. Much simpler simulation models can be made with numbers in a spreadsheet.

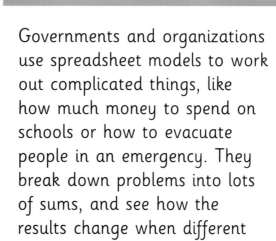

Governments and organizations use spreadsheet models to work out complicated things, like how much money to spend on schools or how to evacuate people in an emergency. They break down problems into lots of sums, and see how the results change when different things happen.

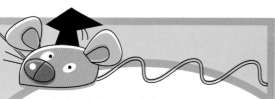

### Working with money

A budget is the money available for a project. Your school has a budget – a fixed amount it can spend on books, teachers, new buildings and so on.

### Budget model

If you plan a party, you might have a budget for that. You can use a spreadsheet to show you how you could spend the money in different ways. This spreadsheet shows how many guests you could have with a £40 budget and two possible menus.

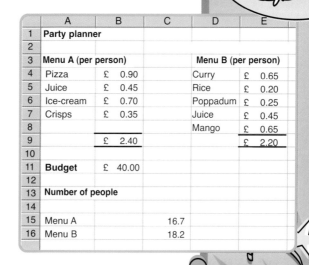

| | A | B | C | D | E |
|---|---|---|---|---|---|
| 1 | Party planner | | | | |
| 2 | | | | | |
| 3 | Menu A (per person) | | | Menu B (per person) | |
| 4 | Pizza | £ 0.90 | | Curry | £ 0.65 |
| 5 | Juice | £ 0.45 | | Rice | £ 0.20 |
| 6 | Ice-cream | £ 0.70 | | Poppadum | £ 0.25 |
| 7 | Crisps | £ 0.35 | | Juice | £ 0.45 |
| 8 | | | | Mango | £ 0.65 |
| 9 | | £ 2.40 | | | £ 2.20 |
| 10 | | | | | |
| 11 | Budget | £ 40.00 | | | |
| 12 | | | | | |
| 13 | Number of people | | | | |
| 14 | | | | | |
| 15 | Menu A | | 16.7 | | |
| 16 | Menu B | | 18.2 | | |

# All change!

One of the main reasons computer models are so useful is that you can make changes and see how things would work out in real life.

## Planning and design

Designers and other professionals often use models to test their plans. For example, an engineer designing a bridge will use a computer model to see what would happen if heavy traffic crossed the bridge, or if a hurricane hit it.

## Using simulations

If you play a simulation game, or if there is a simulation program you can use at school, you can make choices and see what happens as you do different things. For example, a skateboarding simulation game will show you what happens if you skateboard too fast – sooner or later, you'll fall off!

## Planning

People use spreadsheet models to help them make decisions and plan. Imagine a toy company has decided to make a new range of plastic monsters. They know how many monsters they can sell at different prices, so they use a spreadsheet to find out how much money they'd make at each price:

They sell more monsters if they're cheaper – so the model tells them they'll make the most money by selling their monsters at £5.99.

£5.99

| | A | B | C | D | E |
|---|---|---|---|---|---|
| 1 | Price | | Number of sales | | Total |
| 2 | £ 5.99 | | 700 000 | monsters | £4 193 000 |
| 3 | £ 6.99 | | 500 000 | monsters | £3 495 000 |
| 4 | £ 7.99 | | 400 000 | monsters | £3 196 000 |
| 5 | | | | | |

## Change your party plans

On page 19, you can see how to make a spreadsheet for a party budget. But what if you managed to make a cheaper curry for your party? You could change the cost of curry and the spreadsheet would do the sums again.

| | A | B | C | D | E |
|---|---|---|---|---|---|
| 1 | Party planner | | | | |
| 2 | | | | | |
| 3 | Menu A (per person) | | | Menu B (per person) | |
| 4 | Pizza | £ 0.90 | | Curry | £ 0.50 |
| 5 | Juice | £ 0.45 | | Rice | £ 0.20 |
| 6 | Ice-cream | £ 0.70 | | Poppadum | £ 0.25 |
| 7 | Crisps | £ 0.35 | | Juice | £ 0.45 |
| 8 | | | | Mango | £ 0.65 |
| 9 | | £ 2.40 | | | £ 2.05 |
| 10 | | | | | |
| 11 | Budget | £ 40.00 | | | |
| 12 | | | | | |
| 13 | Number of people | | | | |
| 14 | | | | | |
| 15 | Menu A | | 16.7 | | |
| 16 | Menu B | | 19.5 | | |

## How many people?

Or you could work out how much it would cost to have different numbers of people, using each menu:

| | A | B | C | D | E |
|---|---|---|---|---|---|
| 1 | Party planner | | | | |
| 2 | | | | | |
| 3 | Menu A (per person) | | | Menu B (per person) | |
| 4 | Pizza | £ 0.90 | | Curry | £ 0.65 |
| 5 | Juice | £ 0.45 | | Rice | £ 0.20 |
| 6 | Ice-cream | £ 0.70 | | Poppadum | £ 0.25 |
| 7 | Crisps | £ 0.35 | | Juice | £ 0.45 |
| 8 | | | | Mango | £ 0.65 |
| 9 | | £ 2.40 | | | £ 2.20 |
| 10 | | | | | |
| 11 | Budget | £ 40.00 | | | |
| 12 | | | | | |
| 13 | Number of people | | | | |
| 14 | | Menu A | | Menu B | |
| 15 | 5 | £ 12.00 | | £ 11.00 | |
| 16 | 10 | £ 24.00 | | £ 22.00 | |
| 17 | 15 | £ 36.00 | | £ 33.00 | |
| 18 | 20 | £ 48.00 | | £ 44.00 | |
| 19 | 25 | £ 60.00 | | £ 55.00 | |

# Finding patterns

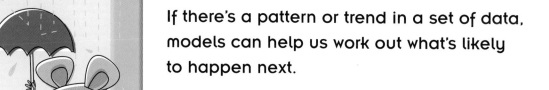

If there's a pattern or trend in a set of data, models can help us work out what's likely to happen next.

## Weather modelling

Weather forecasts are an example of using models to predict what's going to happen. Meteorologists (people who study weather) keep records of the weather and look for patterns. These patterns are used to make computer models that can work out what the weather's likely to do next.

SATURDAY

| | A | B |
|---|---|---|
| 1 | **Times tables** | |
| 2 | | |
| 3 | 1 | 9 |
| 4 | 2 | 18 |
| 5 | 3 | 27 |
| 6 | 4 | 36 |
| 7 | 5 | 45 |
| 8 | 6 | 54 |
| 9 | 7 | 63 |
| 10 | 8 | 72 |
| 11 | 9 | 81 |
| 12 | 10 | 90 |
| 13 | 11 | 99 |
| 14 | 12 | 108 |

## Number patterns

You can use a spreadsheet to see patterns in numbers, too. This spreadsheet shows the nine times table, up to 12 x 9.

You can see that in each of the numbers – 18, 27, 36 and so on – the digits add up to nine:

| | | |
|---|---|---|
| **18** | 1 + 8 | = 9 |
| **27** | 2 + 7 | = 9 |
| **36** | 3 + 6 | = 9 |

But does that always happen?

With a spreadsheet, it's easy to check. You can continue the spreadsheet up to any number you like. You'll find that from 21 x 9, the digits sometimes add up to 18 instead.

# DO IT!

To make the nine times table spreadsheet, you'll need to put numbers counting upwards from 1 in column A. Then in cell B3 put the formula:

**=a3*9**

You can then use an option to 'Copy' or 'Replicate' this cell down the column. When you copy it, the spreadsheet changes the formula so that it's right in each row. So in cell B6, the formula will be:

**=a6*9**

If you wanted the spreadsheet to show the eight times table instead, you'd change the formula in B3 to:

**=a3*8**

and copy this into all the cells in the column.

# Perfect!

If you use a spreadsheet in a project or to present the results of an experiment, make sure it's clear and easy for other people to understand.

## Nice and clear

When you first make a spreadsheet, what you're doing is fresh in your mind, so you might not think you need to label the cells. But later, when you've done some other work, you might not remember what your spreadsheet shows.

A spreadsheet like this, that's just numbers with no titles or labels, won't mean much to you – and it certainly won't make sense to anyone else!

|   | A | B | C |
|---|---|---|---|
| 1 | 03 June | | 3 |
| 2 | 10 June | | 2 |
| 3 | 17 June | | 0 |
| 4 | 24 June | | 1 |

|   | A | B | C | D |
|---|---|---|---|---|
| 1 | Basketball scores | | | |
| 2 | | | | |
| 3 | Match date | | Points we scored | |
| 4 | 03 June | | 3 | |
| 5 | 10 June | | 2 | |
| 6 | 17 June | | 0 | |
| 7 | 24 June | | 1 | |

So remember to add clear, accurate labels like these as you make each spreadsheet.

## Is it right?

As long as you put the right data into a spreadsheet, and give it the right instructions, it will give you the right answers. But if you make a mistake, it will go wrong. Always do a few rough calculations to make sure the answers in your spreadsheet make sense.

Here are some of the reasons a spreadsheet can go wrong:

• You've used the wrong formulas.

• You've made a mistake putting your data into the spreadsheet, like putting numbers in the wrong order or missing something out. (Remember, making a graph can help you spot errors like this.)

• You've mixed up different units (putting some lengths in metres and some in centimetres, for instance).

Always check your work carefully when you put your data in, and when you look at the answers.

25

# Projects to try

Now it's time to put your spreadsheet skills into practice. Here are some fun projects to try out for yourself.

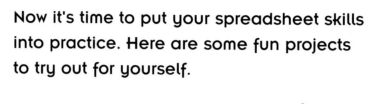

## Leg counter

How many legs are there in your garden? There are hundreds of minibeasts in a garden, and lots of them have legs. You can't count all of them, but you can count a sample and use a spreadsheet to help you estimate how many there are all together!

Don't have a garden at home? You could try this experiment in a school garden or playing field instead.

## Meet the minibeasts

Start by measuring out a one metre square area of your garden, and counting all the minibeasts you can find in it. Make a recording sheet so you can tick them off as you find them:

Spiders /// 
Beetles //
Centipedes //
Worms ////
Slugs //
Flies ///

## Start your spreadsheet

On the computer, open up your spreadsheet program and start a new spreadsheet. Put in the data in the form of labels and numbers, like this:

You'll need to put a formula in the cells in the 'Total legs' column to work out the total number of legs for each type of minibeast.

|  | A | B | C | D | E |
|---|---|---|---|---|---|
| 1 | Minibeast leg counter | | | | |
| 2 | | | | | |
| 3 | | Number found | | Legs each | Total legs |
| 4 | Spiders | 5 | | 8 | |
| 5 | Beetles | 6 | | 6 | |
| 6 | Centipedes | 1 | | 30 | |
| 7 | Worms | 4 | | 0 | |
| 8 | Slugs | 1 | | 0 | |
| 9 | Flies | 2 | | 6 | |
| 10 | Woodlice | 3 | | 14 | |

### How many legs altogether?

At the bottom of the 'Total legs' column, add up all the legs using the 'sum:' formula.

For example, if the number of beetles you found is in cell B5, and the number of legs a beetle has is in D5, the formula you need in E5 is:

**=B5*D5**

## A garden full of legs

Now work out the total for your whole garden. If you counted minibeasts in one square metre and your garden is 70 square metres, you need to multiply your total by 70:

|  | A | B | C | D | E |
|---|---|---|---|---|---|
| 1 | Minibeast leg counter | | | | Total |
| 2 | | | | | |
| 3 | | Number found | | Legs each | Total legs |
| 4 | Spiders | 5 | | 8 | 40 |
| 5 | Beetles | 6 | | 6 | 36 |
| 6 | Centipedes | 1 | | 30 | 30 |
| 7 | Worms | 4 | | 0 | 0 |
| 8 | Slugs | 1 | | 0 | 0 |
| 9 | Flies | 2 | | 6 | 12 |
| 10 | Woodlice | 3 | | 14 | 42 |
| 11 | In one square metre: | | | | **160** |
| 12 | In whole garden: | | | | 11 200 |

In this case, the total goes in cell E12, using the formula:

**=E11*70**

# More projects to try

## Put it in a pie!

Find some information from one of your history topics that you could show as proportions. Put the information into a spreadsheet and use it to make a pie chart. It works best if you choose simple data.

## Henry's wives

Henry VIII of England had six wives, who met with various different fates:

Catherine of Aragon  – divorced

Anne Boleyn          – beheaded

Jane Seymour         – died

Anne of Cleves       – divorced

Catherine Howard     – beheaded

Catherine Parr       – survived

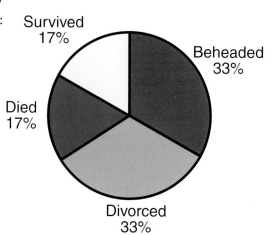

Survived 17%

Beheaded 33%

Died 17%

Divorced 33%

You could draw a pie chart like this from the data:

## More ideas for pie charts

How much of your day do you spend eating, studying, relaxing and asleep?

What do you spend your pocket money on?

What are the favourite colours of the people in your class?

## How many fish?

For this project, see if you can work out how to make the spreadsheet, and what formulas to use.

Imagine you wanted to keep tropical fish. You can get tanks in these sizes:

50cm x 75cm x 50cm
75cm x 100cm x 50cm
75cm x 150cm x 50cm

You can keep five fish in the smallest tank. Can you make a spreadsheet to work out how many fish you could keep in each of the other tanks?

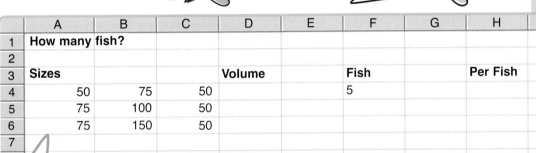

|   | A | B | C | D | E | F | G | H |
|---|---|---|---|---|---|---|---|---|
| 1 | How many fish? | | | | | | | |
| 2 | | | | | | | | |
| 3 | Sizes | | | Volume | | Fish | | Per Fish |
| 4 | 50 | 75 | 50 | | | 5 | | |
| 5 | 75 | 100 | 50 | | | | | |
| 6 | 75 | 150 | 50 | | | | | |
| 7 | | | | | | | | |

**Handy hint**

Put the sizes of the sides in different cells, like this.

**More tips**

Use a formula to work out the volume of each tank, by multiplying the lengths of sides together.

Work out how much space each fish needs, by dividing the volume of the first tank by the number of fish (5).

Find out how many fish can go in each of the other tanks by dividing the volume of each tank by the volume needed for each fish.

## What if? and the National Curriculum

This book will help a child to cover part of work units 3D, 4D, 5D and 6B of the National Curriculum for England and Wales.

The National Curriculum for ICT stresses that ICT should be integrated with other areas of study. This means that a child's use of ICT should fit naturally into other areas of the curriculum. It can be achieved by tasks such as:

• Using a spreadsheet to process data from an experiment or survey.

• Spotting and testing mathematical patterns.

• Using a spreadsheet model to find optimum dimensions for a technology project.

• Using a spreadsheet to sort or filter data from a history or geography project and produce graphs.

Children should incorporate planning, drafting, checking and reviewing their work in all projects. They should discuss with others how their work could be improved, whether ICT methods are the best choice for a given task and how ICT methods compare with manual methods. They should look at ways of combining ICT and manual methods of working.

## National Curriculum resources online

**ICT programme of study at Key Stage 2 in the National Curriculum:**

www.nc.uk.net/nc/contents/ICT-2-POS.html

**On teaching ICT in other subject areas:**

www.ncaction.org.uk/subjects/ict/inother.htm

**ICT schemes of work**
(you can download a printable copy):

www.standards.dfes.gov.uk/schemes2/it/

The schemes of work for Key Stage 2 suggest ways that ICT can be taught in years 3–6.

## Further resources

There is a large number of simulation games on the World Wide Web which you can use with children. Encourage children first to play the game and then to discuss:

• How the simulation is and is not like real life.

• The limitations of the simulation.

• What might happen if they carried out certain actions.

• How a similar simulation might be used for training, experimentation or some other application, besides play.

We advise that you look for and check simulation games yourself to make sure they are appropriate for your children.

# Glossary

**Bar chart**

Chart in which the height of the columns (bars) shows the frequency or number of the thing being counted.

**Cell**

A single rectangle in the grid of a spreadsheet.

**Filter**

To extract a particular type or category of information from a spreadsheet or database.

**Formula**

Instruction used to make a spreadsheet do a sum.

**Line graph**

Graph made by adding lines between plotted points.

**Model**

A pretend version of something real.

**Operator**

Special symbol or word used in a spreadsheet formula or filter.

**Pictogram**

A type of graph or chart that uses little pictures of the objects that are being counted.

**Pie chart**

Chart made by dividing up a circle to show proportions.

**Simulation**

Model of a process or situation used to try things out on a computer.

**Sort**

To arrange information into a particular order.

# Index